Geckos

Photos by David Kenny

Written by Jessica Lee Anderson

Paperback ISBN: 978-1-964078-54-0

To CatAleah, thanks for being so awesome and showcasing geckos as well as other species of reptiles in such a positive light! - JLA

To Heather and Madison, thank you for all your support! - DK

All photos taken by David Kenny apart from: P. 5: kobuspeche (Cape Dwarf Gecko); P. 6: flytosky11 (Gecko Fossil); P. 10: Reptiles4All (Taylor's Fat-tailed Gecko); P: 11: Massimo_S8 (Eyelash Leaf-tailed Gecko); P. 14: Ken Griffiths (Rough Knob-tailed Gecko); P. 15: pr2is (Chahoua Gecko); P. 19: Patrick_Gijsbers (Frog-eyed Gecko); P. 20: fotogaby (Madagascar Giant Day Gecko), Jessica Lee Anderson (Gold Dust Day Gecko); P. 21: Tarikh (Ornate Day Gecko), Corinna Thalies-Feht (Electric Blue Day Gecko), P. 30: sirichai_raksue (Smooth-backed Gliding Gecko); P. 31: Travelarium (House Gecko); P. 33: michaklootwijk (Namib Sand Gecko), David Callan (Chinese Cave Gecko); P. 34: Michael Anderson and Madison Kenny

We would like to thank the following:

Hudson Valley Reptile & Rescue: A reptile rescuer and educator, Brian Parkhurst has been passing on his knowledge of reptiles through educational programs for 22 years. Brian works hard to find homes for reptiles that are surrendered to the rescue. HVR&R is located in Saugerties, New York. https://www.hvreptilerescue.org

Ocean Gallery II Fish and Reptiles: A small, local, family operated pet store in North Plainfield, New Jersey, run by Craig Ost who has over 30 years of experience in reptile keeping. They also specialize in saltwater fish and corals. https://www.oceangallery22.com/

If you are looking to bring a gecko into your family, please consider a reptile rescue, reputable breeder, or a local reptile store that works with reputable breeders. Bringing any reptile into your home is a lifelong commitment.

This Book Belongs to:

_____

Eublepharis macularius

Gekko gecko

Geckos are types of lizards. Unlike other lizard species, geckos can make sounds like barks, chirps, clicks, squeals, and squeaks. They're named geckos because of the sound the Tokay Gecko makes when it vocalizes, "Gecko! Gecko! Gecko!"

Lygodactylus capensis

Gekko gecko

Tokay Geckos also call out, "Tokay!" (Which is how they got their name.) Geckos make noises to attract mates, defend territory, or due to stress or injury. Tokays are one of the largest gecko species. They have powerful jaws and strong bites. Dwarf geckos are some of the smallest species.

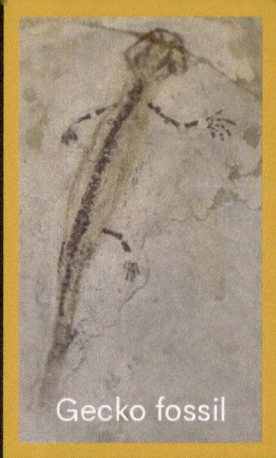

Gecko fossil

Rhacodactylus leachianus

The New Caledonian Giant Gecko is the world's largest living gecko species! Scientists have discovered various gecko fossils that date back to the time of dinosaurs. The New Caledonian Giant Gecko is also known as a Leachie or Leachianus Gecko.

Rhacodactylus leachianus

Like many other gecko species, Leachies have special toe pads that allow them to stick to surfaces. In the wild, they dwell in the rainforest of New Caledonia. Geckos in captivity need specific care and must be kept the right temperature so they don't get too cold or overheat. Some pet geckos may not like to be held.

Eublepharis macularius

Geckos are cold-blooded reptiles, though biologists use terms like ectothermic or poikilothermic. It doesn't mean that geckos have cold blood, but rather that their body temperature varies. Reptiles rely on the environment to stay the right temperature.

Eublepharis macularius

Leopard Geckos store fat in their tails the way camels store fat in their humps. This helps them to survive living in the desert if food becomes scarce. Unlike many other gecko species, Leopard Geckos do _not_ have toe pads. They have eyelids that can blink!

Hemitheconyx taylori

Hemitheconyx caudicinctus

African Fat-tailed Geckos are in the same family as Leopard Geckos along with other species like Taylor's Fat-tailed Geckos. They also store fat in their tails, lack toe pads, and have true eyelids. Fat-tailed gecko species are native to Africa.

Uroplatus phantasticus

Hemitheconyx caudicinctus

Fat-tailed Geckos and many other species like Eyelash Leaf-tailed Geckos can drop their tails if they sense danger or if a predator grabs it (caudal autotomy). The tail drops at break points and wiggles after it falls off. This can distract the predator, helping the gecko to get away. Some species can regrow a tail, but it may look different after.

Toe pad close-up

Correlophus ciliatus

Crested Geckos (or Cresties for short) don't regrow their tail if they drop it. Geckos can survive without a tail, though it could mean less energy or camouflage. It can also cause a change in balance since certain species use their tails to climb. Cresties have toe pads that help them grip, and they even have a toe pad at the end of their tail!

Correlophus ciliatus

Crested Geckos are sometimes called "Eyelash Geckos" because they have fringed crests above their eyes that look like eyelashes. The crests run from their eyes along the top of their heads, necks, and down their backs. Given their size, Cresties and other geckos can get injured if they are dropped or handled roughly.

Rhacodactylus auriculatus

Nephrurus amyae

Gargoyle Geckos are from New Caledonia along with Cresties and Leachies. They are named for the bony bumps on their heads that remind some people of gargoyle statues. Other gecko species like Rough Knob-tailed Geckos have bumps at the end of their tail along with skin lumps. These bumps and lumps are made of skin and connective tissue, not bone.

Rhacodactylus auriculatus

Mniarogekko chahoua

Gargoyle Geckos and species like Chahoua ("Chewie") Geckos are mostly arboreal in the wild, meaning they dwell off the ground in trees and bushes. Pet geckos should have a breathable, appropriately sized enclosure with spots to hide. Some arboreal species need vertical space along with several branches to climb.

Tarentola mauritanica

Crocodile Geckos, or Moorish Geckos, are also mainly arboreal in the wild. Pet geckos need daily care to stay healthy, especially the right amount of water. Geckos can dehydrate if conditions are too dry. If too damp, their enclosures can grow mold, which can lead to respiratory infections.

Tarentola mauritanica

Crocodile Geckos do not have eyelids that can blink. They have a transparent scale on each eye called a spectacle or brille that covers and protects them from injuries. Geckos without eyelids will often lick their eyes to moisturize them and to remove dirt and other things that get stuck to the brille.

Correlophus ciliatus

Gekko badenii

Geckos can have different types and sizes of scales that vary by species. Golden Geckos have small golden scales that cover their body. Like all kinds of reptiles, geckos will shed their skin and scales as they grow and age. They'll eat their shed skin for its nutrients.

Teratoscincus scincus

Gekko badenii

Many gecko species like Golden Geckos and Frog-eyed Geckos are most active at night (nocturnal). They have big, sensitive eyes with large pupils (the dark part of the eye) that allow them to focus when it is dark outside. Several species have camouflage adaptations that help them to blend in at night.

Phelsuma laticauda

Phelsuma madagascariensis madagascariensis

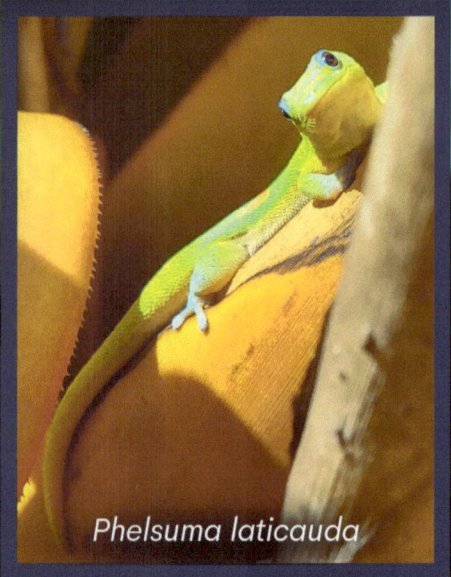

Not all species of geckos are nocturnal! Day geckos like the Madagascar Giant Day Gecko and the Gold Dust Day Gecko are diurnal, or more active during the day. In the wild, they often live in tropical rainforests. They can be challenging to properly care for in captivity and can get stressed if handled.

Lygodactylus williamsi

Phelsuma ornata

Bright colors can help species like Ornate Day Geckos blend into colorful, tropical habitats. The colors of a gecko can also serve as a form of communication to potential mates or possible rivals as they do for Electric Blue Day Geckos. Similar to birds, males are often more colorful than females.

Gekko gecko

Species like Tokays, Cresties, Leopard Geckos, African Fat-tailed geckos, and Gargoyle Geckos are crepuscular, meaning they are most active at dusk and dawn. They avoid the heat of the day and the risk of predators in the deep dark of the night.

Eublepharis macularius

Rhacodactylus auriculatus

Larger reptiles, mammals, and birds of prey pose a threat to gecko species. Geckos have good hearing which allows them to detect possible dangers. Many species have external ear openings that look like holes on either side of their head.

Eublepharis macularius

Gekko badenii

Gekko gecko

Rhacodactylus auriculatus

Whether diurnal, crepuscular, or nocturnal, geckos have extraordinary vision that helps them hunt and avoid predators. Some species can see in color at night and can focus on several objects located at different distances (multifocal vision).

Rhacodactylus leachianus

Like other kinds of reptiles, geckos have two nostrils (nares) on the top of their snout, close to their eyes. They breathe air into lungs by inhaling through their nostrils, similar to you. They have a good sense of smell that they use to find food and communicate.

Correlophus ciliatus

Most geckos eat insects, fruit, and nectar. Several companies make special prepared diets for specific gecko species. Some pet geckos might prefer one brand over another, and they may be picky about whether or not they eat feeder insects.

Correlophus ciliatus

Geckos can become ill due to poor environmental conditions and improper nutrition. They can get conditions like metabolic bone disease and floppy tail syndrome. Smoke, air sprays, chemicals, and more can irritate their sensitive respiratory system. Exotic veterinarians provide care for pet geckos to keep them healthy.

Geckos in captivity have been selectively bred to have genetic mutations in colors, patterns, and sizes called morphs.

Eublepharis macularius

A gecko's morph is determined by the genes and traits passed down from the parents to their babies. Species like Leopard Geckos may undergo color changes as they grow and mature.

Gekko lionotum

Correlophus ciliatus

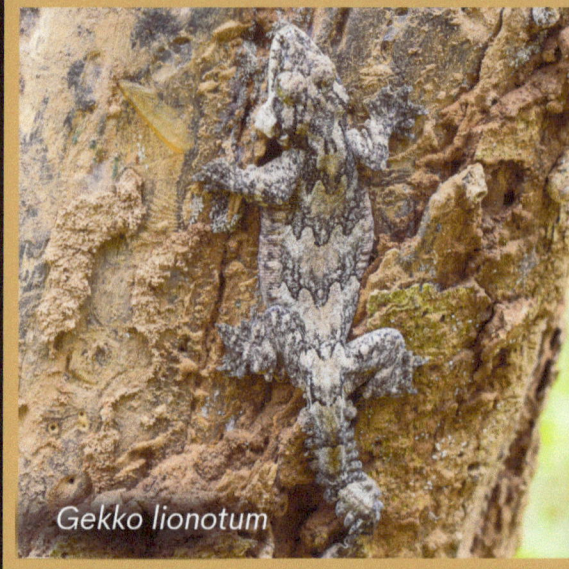

Geckos are known for their acrobatic movements on land and in the air. They have a flexible spine and limbs along with elastic-like connective tissue. Some species can glide in the air because of flaps of skin and webbed feet! Others can briefly run on the water.

Hemidactylus flaviviridis

Correlophus ciliatus

Geckos with toe pads can cling to vertical, slick surfaces (even glass!) because the toe pads are made of many tiny hairs called setae that create a strong, sticky force. The force breaks when the gecko moves. Geckos can climb quickly as they stick and unstick their feet.

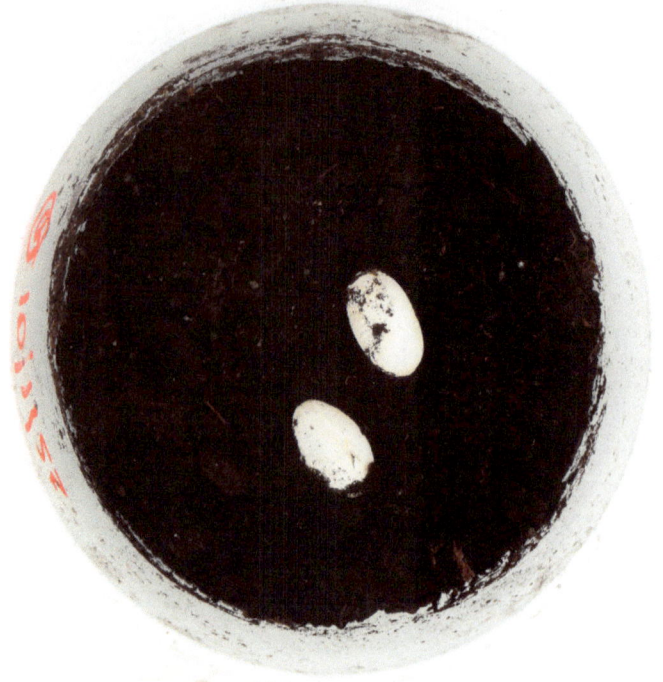

Correlophus ciliatus

Most geckos reproduce by laying eggs, though some species give live birth. Depending on the species, it can take between one month to three months (and sometimes longer) for the eggs to hatch. Babies are fragile and vulnerable, so it can take them a while to feel safe enough to start exploring their environment.

Goniurosaurus hainanensis

Pachydactylus rangei

Eublepharis macularius

There are over 2,000 known gecko species, and researchers continue to make new discoveries! Geckos are found in the wild in a variety of environments like deserts, caves, rainforests, and mountains on every continent except for Antartica. Geckos are popular pets with relatively long lifespans, and they provide companionship to people all over the world.

Jessica Lee Anderson is an award-winning author of over 100 books for young readers including the NAOMI NASH chapter book series and many nonfiction books about reptiles. Jessica loves spending time in nature and exploring the outdoors with her husband, Michael, and their daughter, Ava! You can learn more about Jessica by visiting www.jessicaleeanderson.com.

David Kenny is a photographer from northern New Jersey who enjoys photographing all types of reptiles, amphibians, mammals, and landscapes. His images have been published in numerous books, magazines, calendars and articles. David would like to thank Craig Ost and Brian Parkhurst.

Want to learn more about reptiles? Check out these books:

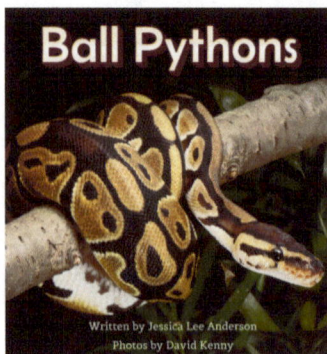

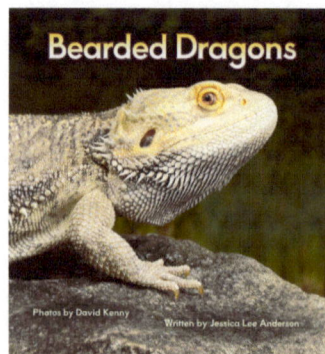

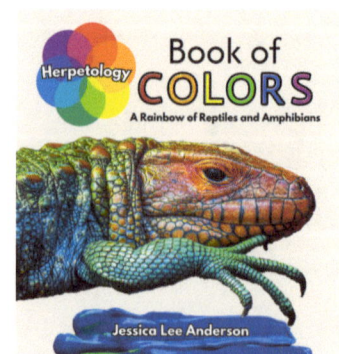

Ball Pythons
Written by Jessica Lee Anderson
Photos by David Kenny

Bearded Dragons
Photos by David Kenny
Written by Jessica Lee Anderson

Herpetology Book of COLORS
A Rainbow of Reptiles and Amphibians
Jessica Lee Anderson

www.ingramcontent.com/pod-product-compliance
Lightning Source LLC
Chambersburg PA
CBHW061144030426
42335CB00002B/98